Rainbows and Brimstone

AF624751

Samantha Cole

BookLeaf Publishing

Presentation by *BookLeaf Publishing*

Web: www.bookleafpub.com

E-mail: info@bookleafpub.com

ISBN: 978-93-95784-51-1

First edition 2022

DEDICATION

I would like to dedicate this book to anyone who lives with an invisible or chronic condition;

You are seen,

You are valid,

You are strong,

You are enough.

ACKNOWLEDGEMENT

I want to thank my soulmate for reading and re-reading my work, and reassuring me that I am a good writer <3 :)

PREFACE

I hope, dear reader, that you found what you came to this book looking for :)

Welcome

Welcome to our brainspace,
please be careful where you tread,
there's hobbies scattered everywhere,
and dark corners that we dread.

There's fields of rainbow flowers,
if you look beyond the mess,
but getting there's impossible,
you'll see we've quite the test.

Anxiety, depression,
and arthritis just to start,
self-actualization,
shouldn't have a panic part.

We've good qualities too,
we're good at making people smile,
we like butterflies and sunshine,
and craft always in freestyle.

Has our tangled mind intrigued you?
Is it worth a spoon?
Don't worry 'bout the red tinge,
you'll learn about it soon...

Her Favourite Thing

When given the chance,
wear a rainbow she will,

a badge of honor,
a bitter pill.

"our cheerful sunshine,"
an ironic play,

dysmorphic eyes
hopeless to sway.

Until that time,
she flies above,

her monstrous thoughts,
to true self love,

lips part to say,
more really to sing,

that rainbows are
her favourite thing.

Apartments

Slippered feet,
dreamy sleep,
carried back to bed...

Adult tears,
she still fears,
that abusive wife she fled...

Kitty waits,
by her dish,
cat men just work late...

A couple here,
adopted twins,
a sweeter side of fate...

Some lights are on,
some lights are off,
some windows curtained tight...

Apartments stand,
lit up and grand,
tall pillars in the night...

A Door

This is the door to my secretest life,
not just of love, but deep red with strife.
A story of pain, too late to back out,
slick from the work, its choking my shout.
Close the void now, in darkness I lay,
trying to nap, dreading the day...

Wish

Wish I was a bird,
with freedom to fly,
my worries lift off,
as I float through the sky.

Wish I could look on,
from my perch on a cloud,
my pain down below,
small and lost in the crowd.

Wish I was a brook,
cool, crisp, full of life,
mind flowing so fast,
no depression in sight.

Wish I could see God,
petulant and proud,
"How could you!? Why me!?"
I'd scream and be loud.

Wish I was a bird,
wish I could look on,
wish I was a brook,
I'd still scream at God.

Pain

My pain is bright red,
my pain is dark black,
that lingers in corners,
and must be bit back.

My pain is a box,
transparent and cold,
forcing my legs,
to buckle and fold.

Pain thick as molasses,
it lingers like oil,
I'm flapping my arms,
just to try and seem normal.

I creak and groan deep,
I wince, sometimes cry,
I'm pounding my fists
in my head screaming why?

Clutching myself,
beaten and done,
I'm somehow still also
expected to run.

I swallow the comments,
I swallow the pain,
and move for my life
with a belly of shame.

Could you do it too?
Disabled and work,
with your partner, your pain,
your shadow from birth?

It's Alright (Verse 1)

Diagnosis, disorder,
I'm sick of this torture,
please leave me alone,
I'm done.

Don't touch me, don't bug me,
especially don't hug me,
please leave me alone,
I'm done.

And I know that's not true,
as I clasp onto you,
sobbing and screaming
and wondering why?

Be mindful I know,
but I just need to show,
all of the damage that is inside,
(that's inside)

It's okay, it's alright,
but we're not getting out
without a fight.

It's okay, just stay strong,
we have the will
to carry on.

It's okay, just believe,
I promise we won't hurt
in our dreams.

Resilient and brave,
only time will heal this pain,
It's alright.

It's Alright (Verse 2)

Anxiety, aching,
I swear I'm not faking,
those looks just heartbreaking,
I tried.

To be calm and typical,
while thinking I'm invincible,
my soul just on fire,
I tried.

And I know my best showed,
but I still have this load,
and I sob and I scream
and I wonder why?

Be patient I know,
I need room to grow,
we must learn to walk before we fly,
(before we fly)

It's okay, It's alright,
we will get used
to clashing fights.

It's okay, we are strong,
and we have the will
to carry on.

It's okay, just believe,
I promise we won't hurt
in our dreams.

Resilient and brave,
I know that we can heal this pain,
It's alright.

ROYGBV

RED is a trainer,
and ORANGE you glad,

that YELLOW is sunshine,
and my rhyming's not bad?

GREEN is a forest,
the colour of calm.

BLUE is the ocean,
It's lapping a song.

VIOLET's a name,
the best colour too.

The bigger the rainfall,
the better the view.

To Be Cute

"Awe, you're so cute!" They readily said,
"But I'm too fat to be cute," my mind fed.

Fat is a size, no personality trait,
cute is a testament to the smiles that you make.

They insist once again, "You are cute!" Sure it's true,
"But I'm too tall to be cute," tears ensue.

Tall is a measurement, no size of your heart,
why do your meters from the ground play a part?

My friends are here now, they're saying the same,
"But I'm too smart to be cute!" I complain.

They spun me around, "Sit down now hun,
who told you that nonsense, you could only pick
one?"

"It's true you have fat,
its true that you're tall,
it's true that you're smart,
but you're cute most of all."

Can I really believe it? My mind in dispute,
I know I'm those things, but I just...

want to believe that I'm cute.

Fate

Do you ever hear whispers,
as they rustle the leaves?

Ever see the signs,
through the tops of the trees?

Do you feel that small hand,
pressed gently to your back?

Urging you forward,
despite the confidence you lack?

It quiets the unease,
that is yelling so loud,

and steps back to the shadows,
so you can feel proud.

It puts you on track,
always before it's too late.

Trust me, my friend,
believe me, It's fate.

Six Haiku's

Bright like a cherry,
Red as any raspberry,
The colour of life.

Orange is tangy
Bigger fruits if it's rainy,
The colour of fun.

Yellow is happy,
A bright, warm, comforting hug,
The colour of smiles.

The valleys and trees,
Are overtaken by green,
The colour of rest.

The rivers and pools,
Plus our sky equals true blue,
The colour of cool.

Violet and purple,
Decorate fields of flowers,
Beauty at it's best.

Ē

Last night when I was fast asleep,
I had the weirdest dream.
I know they're full of make-believe,
but this is what I seen:

The ocean lapping peacefully,
except that is was burgundy,
the sky a deep red travesty,
all else in perfect harmony.

Sitting underneath a tree,
a singing pink anemone,
writing a biography,
looking oh so solemnly.

The hot sand took a casualty,
a fluffy purple bumblebee,
it's buzzing oh so pitifully,
the beach folk watch obnoxiously.

I'm allowed movement finally,
and start to run aggressively,
towards the boat that's painted green,
I hope to take across the sea.

But before I have a strategy,
I wake up quick and chokingly,
a shark had just spontaneously,
attacked my legs ferociously.

Social Anxiety

Big crowds are the worst,
there's more people to see,
they're constantly watching,
it's all eyes on me.

Every step closely counted,
each movement assessed,
eyes follow me always,
they must think I'm a mess.

My voice just betrayed me,
and I stuttered a bit,
I'll think of it nightly,
never let me forget it.

I tripped up the stairs,
just one normal thing,
but their eyes are upon me,
stressing me taught like a bowstring.

They just see my flaws,
my mind screams out too loud,
you have nothing to offer,
it threatens and growls.

Depression, anxiety,
both social and general,
why does it just
make me feel so expendable?

Everyday

Every damn day,
it just feels the same,
upsetting and sad,
and coloured with pain.

I'm grasping at straws,
for any gram of dopamine,
meanwhile on a pain scale from one to ten,
I'm at an eighteen.

The scars are internal,
and chronically sore,
but no-one else sees them,
and I've done this before.

Pretend to be "good",
while I'm searing inside,
faking it and making it,
while my brain is preoccupied.

I just want an inch,
to stretch and be me,
without the restraints,
and my disorders as company.

Don't tell me life's hard,
I got it, okay?
I'm always in pain,
and it sucks everyday.

Tommy In His Ways

Tommy in his ways,
he always runs and plays.
he eats a lot of cat food,
by the passing days.

If Tommy didn't eat,
and if Tommy didn't play,
then that just wouldn't be,
Tommy in his ways.

Fibromyalgia

Forgetting what it's like to not be in pain.
I'm doing okay, I don't want to complain.
Bones aching so badly I just want to cry.
Reminding myself everyday why I try.
Opting to stand where no one will see me.
My shit mental health refuses to free me.
Yearning for normalcy.
All alone in my emergency.
Legs hurting, things burning.
Guts always churning.
I want to get off this ride.
All I want to do is hide.

Small Town

My small town is tiny,
I'm sure you'll agree,
but did you know really,
it's the best place to be?

The forests are bursting,
to forage and eat,
where else can you find that,
two minutes by feet?

The poutine is cheesy,
the ice cream is creamy,
the best treat in summer,
strawberry slush puppies!

The sunsets are messy,
great washes of colour,
the soundscape is sloppy,
the sirens particular.

Hands down the number one
garage sale community,
but the homeless are burdened,
the poor short on opportunity.

Our downtown is quaint,
but watch who you walk by,
or get stabbed at midday,
at least the hospital's nearby.

The people are unique,
from all walks of life,
but the white ones are racist,
or are dude bros from Goodlife.

The last time I heard,
heart of gold was our maxim,
but did you know we're only worth,
the gold under our houses?

So many good people,
just needing some scraps,
but meanwhile were barely big enough,
to be put on a map.

My small town is tiny,
I'm sure you'll agree,
but did you know really,
it's my small town that needs me?

Favourite colour

When asked favourite colours,
it's rainbow! I shout,
it is the best ever,
there's really no doubt!

What colour is everything,
all at the same time?
What colour looks better,
when stacked up in a line?

The order's important,
to the text of this colour,
ROY G BV's easy,
with a sentence to refer.

If it's easier this way,
you can lay out the primaries,
and then go and squish between each
together, their capabilities.

But I'm making this hard,
I just get so excited,
to talk about all of the colours
that white light shed.

I swear that it's magic,
that a short burst of rain,
can send the sky dancing,
full of colour unrestrained.

You might call me extra,
or even bizarre,
but I'll always wear rainbows,
and feel like a star!

Depression

My depression is blue,
not bright like spring skies,
more like the drab colours,
of tearful goodbyes.

It sucks all my joy,
and makes still the waters,
when I just want to surf,
and be my own author.

It bridles my craft,
and strangles my dexterity,
it makes me believe,
that I suck at my mastery.

It lurks in my subconscious,
stamping out all the positives,
when their right in my face,
turning them into opposites.

My depression is sure,
that we have no friends,
and crying in bed,
is all it recommends.

There's too many reasons,
to sit and be sad,
I'm chronically ill,
my mental health just all bad.

I hurt all the time,
and have panics randomly,
I'm trying to live,
but I'm surviving frantically.

I can't blame myself,
for being so blue,
it's just my genetics,
but I want a break too.

Goodbye

My insecurities are showing,
doubting how this is going,

I know the books done,
but I've only just begun,

to tease out the pain,
and heal what remains,

was I sharing too much,
using my grief as a crutch?

Should I cover it up,
once again build up,

the wall that I made-
I'm off topic in spades.

I think I might have,
some more mind work to do,
maybe I'll do it,
inside a book two?

Thank you.

www.ingramcontent.com/pod-product-compliance
Lightning Source LLC
Chambersburg PA
CBHW051751130826
49812CB00033B/1095
9789395784511